GIBBET LANCE

Jon Tait

abuddhapress@yahoo.com

ISBN: 9798338785713

Jon Tait 2024
©™®

Alien Buddha Press 2024

In the beginning, there was Cheviot.
Bubbling up from the core in molten magma chambers
and blasted out to thunder flash grey skies
orange and red, columns of ash
and pyroclastic clouds;
a violent birth ripped and torn from the soil
then oozing, crystallising, sizzling into the sea.

Cheviot, a bog round a mound,
hills cooled from the inferno
into hard volcanic dolerite,
worn smooth by the boots of hikers
as a pebble washed up on North Sea surf.

A green blanket of lumps and bumps
cast out to comfort like a Granny's quilt
pulled up tight around the neck
with frost crystals on the windows,
the coal in the Aga glowing
as the embers under earth.

*

A people daubed in red ochre
Scavenging shellfish on the beaches at Embleton
under the Whin Sill, the Whin Stone,

Chipped and flaked flint into arrowheads
Dropped in sand and picked up delighted
4,000 years later
by a midden ratching father and son,
celebrating the small victories.

*

Hill of the Goats, the Bell,
An old bearded Billy patrolling the steep side's flanks
topped of tumbled pink rocks that once glistened in sunshine,
weather washed and turned over,
as the wild herd appears silently and wanders past,
the youngster's kicked hinds and weak bleats.

The turned horn of shepherd's crooks,
Clouds poured like milk in the blue skies
Gate posts of Ad Gefrin carved with goat's heads
and the memories of Anglo-Saxon Kings
echo like the reverberation in their great wooden halls
around empty countryside.

Listen
and the Bell sounds in the wind.

*

Chipped circles into rock,
by hillforts cut into turf and
raised by wooden stakes.
An interpretation of stars
of the universe,
of carved antlers and a sword blade
forged from a mix of metals;
fiery orange heat melting steel and iron,
hammered glowing and pliable.
Adding the female to the male,
the snake eating its tail,
the eternal yin to yang,
quenched and tempered by the union of bodies
entwined and locked together smooth as a mortise and tenon,
damp as rain and hard as dolerite.

Genetic codes passed on from women soft and curved,
the mix in the Borders slipping invisible
down family lines forgotten in time,
fox-coloured follicles in a beard,
on a chest.

Neither Scottish nor English,
but a broth of both,
a hell-fire double helix fired in a sky

black with falling arrows.

*

The Imperial wall
A Caesarean scar across a green belly,
cut stone blocks from quarries
and laid flat.

Build your small temples to Mithras
in badger dips of Brocolitia where the wind howls;
There is no sun here.

Just ask your Glorious Ninth
vanished in peat bog with rusted helmet and shield,
disgraced Standard depressed
in the wet earth on purple heather moor
with sheep tracks sinking in the black,
a curlew nesting in long grass.

Write home for more socks,
Tell tales of a lost legion.

*

A hare mad leaping up in cropped corn fields
to bound in drunken lines
with the weak rays
of the rising sun,
through morning grass sodden in dew
and a low mist lifting to reveal Bamburgh Castle
sat atop the red rock.

Old Bebbanburg
Stands stiff as stone slowly warmed,
the waves rolling into the sand
and dune tops whipped by the winds.

Great golden Angle knots
and animistic scenes;
a culture of nature,
of two stags buried standing up.

Red Bamburgh
square and squat, the capital,
the kingdom of Northumbria,
red as a fox disappearing into the trees
Eilaf the monk
who stole the cheese

and became Dodd.

*

Monks from Ireland and Scotland
that spread the word
of a joiner from Bethlehem
who was nailed to a cross
in a land of yellow dirt and dust
and strange tongues.

Devotion
Divinity

The illuminated writing on great Gospels
Plundered not by Vikings
But by the South, by London,
By Arts Councils and Libraries
And men in suits who
Think they know best.

The island brings solitude.
I am Cuthbert in my brown robes of itchy cloth,
arms outstretched to welcome my ducks
all downy and feathered
waddling over black rocks wet with spray,

and I savour the silence.

*

Sigurd Snake-in-the-Eye announced his arrival
in a pile of bones shaking like sea shells
and the slow worms that slithered on their bellies
shining and silvery as the stars
all disappeared under rocks blackened by fire
and into the crevices of castles.

Lithe, limbless lizards with flicking forked tongues
that told tales of the Saints;
of Aidan, of Wilfrid and Cuthbert,
the eider ducks and the smash of angry white water
against pillars of black rock stained white with guano,
the high shrieks of sea birds,
the settling of spuggies in the trees at roosting,
great murmurations of starlings blackening the sky
in ever shifting masses.

The devil in a kilt of torn tartans
and it could be the summit of Skiddaw
on slippery black rocks inside low rain clouds
thick as cotton wool,
the mist hanging heavy over the Tyne;

snaking slowly down narrow steep winding nicks
and across darkened cobbles,
the weak glow of streetlights in the gloom
barely illuminating
dim as smudged orange halos in the grey.
Bridges curved and riveted in cold steel
looming large as mountains
sensed on a rain-lashed trail
high above the slow-moving river
lapping gently against the stone of the quayside.

Sigurd Snake-in-the-Eye's gan hyem to the bairns,
the voices that never lost the Scandinavian lilt,
to follow a path through the streets
as sure as a boggy single-track in the wilderness
with a potential drop into the void at either side,
feeling that you could fall spinning into nothingness,
an electric anticipation crackling in the air
tinged with excitement and yet foreboding,
charged with thunderous intent,
quickening the step,
the silence of the City in the darkness of night
all-enveloping as Tyneside sleeps
under the blanket of fog at Stupid O' Clock.

The thump of heavy machinery

at Swans or Armstrong Vickers all tucked in,
only the sound of the work boots echoing back from the emptiness
like a couple of pieces of four-by-two
being slapped together
in the dusty confines of a joiner's shop.

Somewhat sullen in his solitude.
Sigurd Snake-in-the-Eye summoned his brothers
From the boiling sea;
The Sons of Ragnar Lothbrok,
Thrown down in a pit of serpents;
Bjorn Ironside, Ivar the boneless,
Pride of the Great Heathen Army.

Oh, Odin,
You big, bearded behemoth,
The North Men are coming
To smash up your stadiums,
And ravage your women.

And it's Dane Law
On the beaches at Bamburgh
And Lindisfarne is a smoking wreck.

Thor's hammer in the heather

The slow worm's orange eye as a bird
Unblinking in perpetual low winter sun.

*

A pine marten in Rothbury Forest
disturbed in his canopy of leaves
by the clank of metal
as William Wallace
and his hordes assemble.

Butcher a deer
and rest under stars with
warm venison in the belly tonight.

When Wallace's body
was chopped up into four pieces
after he'd been hung and drawn
down in London,
his right arm came to Newcastle
and his left arm to Berwick,
rotted on the gibbet
in rusting chains.

Not enough flesh
to fill Northumberland's hungry belly.

*

So tell me tales of the Northumberland Night.

Of crows cackling disdain,
scratching on a steel breastplate with clawed feet
smooth as snakeskin
to feast on soft eyes,
to peck sockets' clean to bone
white as twisted trees bleached by the sun
in moonlight.

Who dare disrupt supper?
The bright banners torn and stamped into mud,
ground churned and sodden in offal
steaming up into mist.
beaks and feathers congealed in bold blood
soaked into Harry Hotspur's soil,
sold off to the highest bidder.

*

Jerry Charleton
stepped over the bodies of dead gaolers
felled by the plague
at Berwick.

Jerry Charleton
walked out of opened oak and iron doors
when they heard his family were riding
on Hexham.

We are the buffer zone,
the War region,
the killing fields.

Marched over by armies, butchered and bled.
We are the Border, the invisible line.
The Debateable lands;
a crown woven from wiry wool
and blackberry thorns
by the hands of farm labourers,
freestone quarrymen.

*

Mere stone cannot contain me. I'll bide time in these walls on cold volcanic black rising over the City of filth and fear as a stag in the green forest, breath billowing from nostrils in the morning dew by a stream and blink in the same strange light that breaks through leaves as window bars. The chill touch of cut rock sullen as a dead lover, I kiss my broken lips to the grains for moisture and solace. Son of David Scott of Tushielaw, son of Scotland, this red lion.

There's no land but my land.

Gentlemen, I bid you adieu.
Come visit me in Ettrick sometime.

*

A solitary ash tree bowed in the wind by broken stones hewed from a quarry, scar on the belly of the soil, pressure whipping over heather moorland. Cry of the curlew. The sad, swinging legend of a spectral gallows rope; hockle on the Heart of Midlothian, glistening wet with soft rain. The stinking tollbooth, the grey walls of Edinburgh, sick, sullen smack of an axe.

Pay up John Brown. Pay up Andrew Thorbrand.

I'm here to collect the black meal, boys.

*

I didn't hear any complaints when I was hacking my way through the billhooks at Flodden; smashing steel against bone, leather jack splashed in blood, the cannon smoke drifting over the boggy ground, colourful flags and agonised screams.

Now assembled in ghostly ranks each September, drizzle on the grey dawn grass at Branxton Hill, the winds whispering a roll-call of Buccleuch, of Douglas and Maxwell, the chaffinches chattering in hedgerows.

A homage to dead kinsmen in the form of a badger or fox concealed by the dyke back, among the tangled brambles and nettles, while a lone piper skirls a lament at the monument.

No, you didn't want to put my neck in the tight grip a noose then. To see me kicking and choking and dangling like a bundled fly in a web damp with dew.

They only came for me when it suited you.

*

The King of Thieves is a nickname,
not a title,
and to be honest it's a shame that you take it all so seriously.
Don't dig too deep.
There's no great meaning that we keep
to our daft monikers.

There's a lad called Foul Thumbs
and do you reckon when he comes home
he gets called that?

We do it for the banter,
for the crack,
taking the piss out of blokes
like Davy the Lady
and auld Black Jack.

My wife calls me Adam;
my father, Buggerlugs.

*

Mist follows rivers down valleys
set by the milky way.
crash of animals in woods
the disturbed sheep

Faces faded to grey as cancer patients
in the absence of light
under glinting steel helmets
washed out/ the illusion of fear

& the winds whisper through tangled heather
Copper stills, heat on the breath
a broken spear.

The night a parable of our magic circle
Pagan chant, Viking lore, texture of snakeskin.

*

There is no wall of concrete and graffiti here.
No barbed wire or sentry boxes, swinging searchlights,
or the wail of a siren.

Just the gently rise and fall of the Cheviots,
the crash of water at Hen Hole,
boggy trails up the Muckle hill.

Big skies. Startled pheasants garbled scalding.
I jettison mad seed into warmth by Bloodybush Edge
And no-one hears the sobbing.

Bring me my rim of Spanish steel.
Bring my Scottish blade.

Saddle up and ride the border,
Slap the sturdy flank of steaming, bellowing beef.
Drive sheep along our father's paths.

For the blackness of your cells
are no blacker than my heart.

*

And the horse hooves rage with wild fury over the mosses,
and the sky turns black,
threatening thunder over high green hills.

And Johnnie Armstrong is ripped from the rope
and embraced by cold soil,
and the crows are cackling in the trees like old women.

And I'm next.
I'm next.

Hot rock and the crack of blackened wood
fired in ferocity and we're riding again.

Into the mist,
into the mountains of loose scree,
a belly full of retribution bitter as bile.

*

Hands calloused as oak bark grip the smoothed wooden block, worn rough by wielding a sword and the farm, the cows at Tushielaw bowed heads and lowing in the corner of a field, the tactile memories of running slowly over the smooth curves of soft breasts stop the knuckles from turning white and I'm thinking: make it a clean strike, you bastard, and hoping I don't shit myself when the blow comes. Hell, I've got a reputation to upkeep. And when the head turns grey on the spike, and the blood's dried brown in matted hair, and the lifeless eyes gawp into rainy skies from the tollbooth, remember this: I only ever did what I had to do. Now someone hold those hands and lead me to the light.

*

Adam Scott, the King of Thieves,
beheaded by his Monarch.
Adam Scott, a transparent apparition
the colour of trout scales
appearing in the fields of yellow corn
as a silent grim;
The black mark.

I was born here and I'll die here,
in my boots or in my bed, whatever.
The Border is my home.
The green bracken, purple rolling moors of heather,
the fields and rivers,

the ghosts of the past,
shadows of hill fort dwellers and nibble-fingered flint knappers.

I'm not leaving.

I'd rather lie deid in the soft brown earth of my own soil
and rot with the bones of my ancestors than flee,
the worms and beetles ingesting my soft flesh
and a little piece of me will live on in them.
Eaten by a bird then ejected onto the soil in a white splat
along with seeds to grow roots tough as sinew;
to live anew in the weak sun and soft rains.

For the Border land is my land,
the comforting embrace of a mother to her warm breasts,
the air sweet as milk.

I will not go.

*

I strung up men from the trees around my tower, it's true,
a blackened and bloated fruit buzzing fresh with flies,
rotting flesh pulsing with maggots.

The stench of death ripe in the air at Tushielaw, decayed as dead rabbits.

Rib cage, gristle and grime as the crows pecked slimy eyes from their
sockets
and squabbled, flapping in ferocity at a cawed dawn.

The swinging creak of rope on bark
and the perpetual motion of a corpse in chains
slowly spinning in the breeze
a soundtrack to my hellish integrity.

*

I'm a broken man;
outlawed from the clan,
cut loose to flee into the highland wastes.

The last of the long riders,
last in a line of faces swimming in the ether,
white and smoky;

Johnny Armstrong of Gilnockie,
the dark mark around his neck,
eyes rolled back in their sockets,
each face a star twinkling in the night sky.

Others with eyes and mouths stitched shut
with thick red thread,
disembowelled and limbs hacked off,

dragging terrible gangrenous injuries
across a stone floor on bloody stumps.

Black scabs split revealing fresh red.
Bruises turned brown, blue and purple
as the sky before a storm.

Shattered spears and gouged helmets;
Geordie Burn, Cuddy Lyle Robson,
Ill Drooned Geordie Nixon, Archie Fire-the-Braes,
rising with a sad groan of voices,
low whispered moans of injustice,
pleading innocence,
at once both bitter and defiant,
a distant foghorn over the sea;

And he is there,
Adam Scott of Tushielaw,
the King of the Border,
beckoning me forward
into their smothering, hypnotic embrace
of clawing hands,
the ghostly legacy of the great border raiders.

We all find a bed in the grave at the end.

*

Northumberland is my world.
The scree slopes and valleys and mountain tracks secret to my soul;
the weak bleat of lambs, grey veins of drystone walls
and lonely curlew cries over wet lands with tufts of tough grass
map a depiction of my immortality.

For so long as the sun rises in rain showers
over the igneous outcrops, we'll be on the Border.

I cannot leave.

Bred to the hills and high heather moors,
bred to a Clan and Chieftain command,
of orange daylight fading golden over autumnal colours
and an incessant gurgle into deep brown pools.

Born out of flame and battle axe,
pulled from my mother kicking and screaming
with blood in my eyes,
and that was the way I'll go;
And while some fall from a sword strike,
some from the piercing of arrows
and others drooned under the weight of booty
in the Tweed or Till,

swirling, bubbling blue as the sky then descending into darkness
in weightless, graceful fall,
I'll see you on the spectral battlefield.
Aye ready.

*

Adam Scott of Tushielaw;
a headless rider galloping over the heather moors
on a dark stallion with a white star on the forehead,
the land charred and blackened in his wake.

Adam Scott, King of Thieves,
can't you hear the terrible rumble,
the hooves tearing up the turf behind?

The distant drum roll off in a patchwork of green fields
like a Roman mosaic across the hills of Northumberland
picking up the pace in approaching,
the dreadful vibrations thumping in your chest
and echoing through the chamber
waking bolt upright and sweating in the sheets.

Adam Scott the childhood bogeyman;
if you don't behave, Adam Scott will come and get you.
Where's my mam? She's run off with Adam Scott.

Long nights of spooky stories with older brothers
as the winds battered old stone walls
and howled a hooly up the lonnen.

The King of the Border was always there.

An omen of bad luck
akin to seeing a lolloping hare in the early morning dew of a crop field
or a vision of blood dripping like rain off bowed grass.
Families at feud for generations.

The legacy of our forefathers.

*

Chuck me doon Haddock's Hole
Snug as a sett, rolled tight in dark earth,
the smell of decaying leaves and rotting vegetation
cling to cold sandstone, the drip of the sea.

Out of the blackness to soar like a hawk
over Northumberland, a wilderness of tangled heather,
of grey boulders deposited by receding ice caps,
of boggy peat lands, of holiday lets
and a commuter belt

tight as a noose around the neck.

*

Adam Scott, King of Thieves,
a beckoning phantasm emanating
from the bastle walls of grey stone,
decomposed skin in folds as if held in warm water,
tattered clothing like a manikin to scare the crows off the crop seeds;
the sense of great injustice and transience reeking
from a rotting corpse with a bloody stump for a neck.
A terrible phenomena spilling centipedes,
sheep scab, beetles.

Retribution for years of bad blood between families,
a penitence for the preservation of pestilence.

Give back Buccleuch's grandfather's sword,
Give back the land to till and toil.

*

It was the day the birds stopped singing; sullen starlings savour silence - tell me the secrets of the black sun, seductive maiden of Hollywood, covered in tattoos from her breasts to her toes. There are swallows, a pin-up, and an angel on majestic curves above her black lace bra. Staring in childlike wonder at the neon man in the window, flesh covered in barnacles and drowned out at sea. Scream of grey gulls in first flight, sand and brine.

You are more than a name; you're a cup and ring carved into sandstone on a lonely hillside, a pink and silver-flanked salmon leaping wild white waters of Tyne. You're the smell of pine and soil in fat summer rain, the swish of the cornfields, the bark of a deer. You're a Viking on grey seas sighting land, a glinting penny on the pavement; a bundle of somatic cells, a swirl of atoms. You are the view over a calm lake from the top of a mountain. You're a waterfall tumbling down into a black pool. You're a sperm burying into an egg and a million stars glinting in the black. You're the northern lights swirling green and blue, an osprey chick in a nest of sticks and fish guts, the connections on a gleaming neon computer circuit board. You're a Saxon cross in a market square, a spiky split horse chestnut case among the headstones. You're a bundle of X chromosomes as well as Y, a twisting ladder. You're the red sky at night. You have the blood of legends in your heart, pumped by electric pulses. You're a flash of lightning, a tic on the back of a mouse, the bacterium Treponema pallidum. You are a grey stone on an old cairn. You are the Deoxyribonucleic acid of The King of Thieves – vengeance and fire, a badger curled asleep in the dark coolness of a woodland sett. The memories of a valley lost underwater.

You're a borderer and you're coming home; back over Solway mud to the embrace of kin snug as a feathered nest in a blaeberry bush, history pages brittle and curled by flames and smoke faint as the perfume on a passing girl on a railway platform inhaled in turning. For my face is your face, a sepia photograph turned over into the cold light of the West that's warmed by the glow of red brick and sandstone at sunset to catch angles, your face; my face; across the years and the generations you live on and you've come home - back to where you belong, unconsciously moving like geese over grey marshland. The whoosh of wings, drawn home to hills etched in our bone marrow, our DNA, turn out the lights, you're coming home.

*

Salt on wet boards, barnacles on a figurehead,
and the North Sea now calm but untamed
to rush up on sand, to beat stone into submission
as the waves whisper the names Admiral Collingwood,
Grace Darling, in tight streets of small villages.
the lobster pots on the harbour
kippers smoked in oak shavings in oily walls
choking and black with tar,
rock breakfasts, buckets and spades, penny floaters,
trawler engines putting out as seagulls' shriek
and the ghosts in oilcloths look on.

The silver sides of fish slipping out of nets,
crabs and starfish in rockpools,

the swish of tough grass atop dunes.

I am the sea
I wash away dreams
that float like oil on water.

*

Emily Wilding Davison
Tried to pin a sash
On the King's horse
And was trampled under hoof.

A lion in yellow sandstone rampant.
They don't call us the Fighting Fifth for nothing –
white hackles dipped in battlefield blood.

Silks glinting in the sun
as each shod foot fell in appalling symmetry
to pound a reckoning for the people;
to those of the sword, strong-willed
and swift to retaliate when provoked.
Sired from great riding surnames;
idle and arrogant in the certainty of birthright
to lift horse and do battle,
right hands unblessed by a Christening.
wild and heather-hardened,

blunt as worn mill stones
set in a converted bastle
with an Audi replacing a tractor
in the drive.

*

Bobby Shaftoe's silver buckles
no longer shine like spurs served up for dinner
and Capability Brown's lines are all crooked.

Northumberland, a miner's lamp and helmet,
a bailer twine belt and a broken gate;
Wellington's pulled out of muck around a water trough,
the splatter of cow's muck and slurry tinging the air.

The herring shoals are gone, the coal seams mined out,
heavy equipment left to rust in dank darkness
and the shepherd on his quad bike
glints as a Kingfisher's feathers in low sun over hillsides.

The greenery at sunset
caught in a corn field glow
by new houses that locals can't afford.
A stoat drags a rabbit into a drystone wall,
a trout takes a fly

and flops into the pool
with a ripple.

*

In the end, there'll be Cheviot,
Rising like a whale's back from marsh,
the water
dark as brown ale.

And Adam Scott appearing
like a Brocken spectre
on a ridge above the valley
in full battle gear,
a brazen glove hung from a spike
still no-one dares take down.

Face hoary and lucent as spent adder skin,
a daft little lop-sided grin,
lined small eyes and wrinkled nose,
defiant as old Cheviot.

To sow seeds in fresh plough lines,
curl weeds round blue billboards
graffitied with his name.

To burn your fields of wheat.

*

The clock and click of a corbie
with grey head like a hangman's hood
clawed feet on dyke copers, tipped by beast,
to chatter and gossip
and spit venomous lies,
beak jutted forward, eyes brown as Tweed
or Kale in flood
upturned under lids,
seeking carrion, to feast on
a body strung in chains
high on exposed moorland.
Corvus corone, glimmered as jasper
all deep blue and purple
in the first light of morning;
wings spread like fingers and leap
to craa and curse
the bare wood of a gibbet.

*

It's better to have a wife's legs
wrapped around your neck

tighter than a noose;
the soft touch of warm skin
tops the burn of coarse rope.

pretty hazel pupils
shadowed by a hood,
dark hair shook free,
intensity of gaze and wanted all the more
to taste and inhale honey and heather deeply,
run hands calloused to touch
from digging and hewing
over curves as the Cheviots.

the fire that flushes cheeks pink,
flighty as a thoroughbred,
like the flames of a farm thatch,
over the shoulder,
forgotten.

*

A bull grabbed by the horns
and grappled to the ground,
turn the bull again to be cast in bronze,
to stand on hard stone in Hawick.
The sons of William Rule
who saved The Bruce from a gorging,

stood tall and became Turn-e-Bull
in towers on high hills;
Fat Lips, grab a girl
and kiss her on entering,
grab sheep and drive them home
through valleys wet with drizzle
to Wauchope in the wilds
above Kielder,
the fields hidden in low mist, no skies
but TV static, where wild men's laughter
bounces back and won't travel with them
across the invisible line.

*

Ka' handed,
we build towers
with spiral staircases
turned anti-clockwise,
sword hilts clashed on stone,
knuckles scraped and scarred
against sedimentary rock
cut square and laid heavy;
sprung on heather
fleet as new lambs,
the game is to accumulate wealth,

collect titles for your crimes,
add a wing, lay more stone,
and if the money runs short
sell a Caravaggio,
build executive housing on spare land,
up the rent for carpets thick as grass,
interiors gilted and bourgeois,
and gawped at by Yanks.

*

Flodden in the rain.
A faint smell of peat smoke
coming off the damp clothes
of men arrayed around
in full battle gear;
the clank of metal,
preparing weapons.

Such a gathering
of the Scottish Border clans
on a darkest day,
pulling in great lungfuls of air
to settle the nerves and steady.
The Teviotdale, Eskdale
and Liddesdale men,

all thieves of great repute,
from the highest of Lairds
to the humblest yeomen,
handing over horses
to lead the opening charge
on foot down the slopes of Branxton hill
at the smaller English army
amassed on the gentler rise below.

A low murmur of grumbling,
the Borderers preferring
to fight on horseback as light cavalry,
rather than use the long,
cumbersome pikes
they'd been handed.

But with King James IV watching on
from the great mass of Highland warriors
assembled alongside them,
they had reputations to uphold
and in what seemed a blur
they were running down the slope,
a jog at first then picking up the pace,
caught up in the charge,
battle screams ringing in the head,
an animalistic and unfamiliar sound

emanating from the throat,
sword drawn and ready.

As the front row ripped
into the English right flank,
it caused carnage;
hacking and stabbing alongside kinsmen,
splashed with warm blood
and tasting hot pennies and brine
in the mouth.

A fight totally different
to the personal threat
and practiced violence of reiving;
the purest human desire for survival.
To kill or be killed.
The English falling all around
wounded by terrible hacking gashes,
helmets being split with the force of blows
and skin being torn and ripped apart by steel,
the brown soil of Northumberland bogged in blood,
agonised screams and confused shouting
among the din of the battle.

It's not something you forget
and on nights those faces

invade dreams,

smashed and bloodied,

carved and cut up

raw as butchery.

Bloody Branxton,

where King James was sliced open

and killed in a bog under English billhooks

along with most of his nobles

and the bulk of the clergy.

Falling in the stinking mud,

hands raised to protect his face,

the agony of arrow strikes

and the brutal bludgeoning of blows.

The Northumbrian mosstroopers

robbed the English camp

while they were fighting;

went back to loot the Scottish camp too,

as their army lay decimated

in pools of mud and blood

with limbs hacked off,

but the Teviotdale riders

had beaten them to it.

*

Get yourself away to Ireland
Micky nae-lugs
and divn't come back.

Away and sup porter
black as tar or the hair of navvies
in a road crew at Twice Brewed,
long out of Cavan, or Navan,
or Cork,
striding up to the wood of a bar worn smooth
by the elbows of drinkers in a brown workman's Mac
to mumble and gesture,
rattle down coins and knock back a pint
in two gulps,
more coin, another pint in the gullet,
then back to the windy pick, the dust in the throat,
the raging thirst.

Get off and be gone,
scabs on the sides of your heid
so they know you steal cattle
as blatant as a birthmark.

*

Dick the Devil's bairns
a crew sent from Hel,
huge breasts unfettered
black and blue as fresh bruising
by a subterranean shore of bodies
washed up and fish eaten,
that crossed fast flooded rivers
and burst open oak doors
with battle axe and wrecking bar.

Or hell, the red horns and flames
licked from fired farms, the pitchforks,
smell of saltpetre harsh in the nose,
a cross on fire and you're crucified,
hanging limp as a wet sock from a washing line
with a face grey as work underpants,
the broken shape of an old brock
hit on the roadside, forlorn,
or the skies over Annandale driven with rain.

chuck salt in a fireplace
to gliff the devil,
cut yourself with a spear
so Hel thinks you died

on the battlefield.

*

A peezle, a pintle,
Willie Hall's on the pull again,
out tupping in hay sheds,
to settle old feuds with a marriage
or murder,
to woo an enemy's daughter,
or wife,
all fresh-cheeked and blushing
eyes shooting death glares at first
'til he'd charmed her.

no guilt at the dalliances,
the exhilaration keeping him
going back for more,
girls coming so hard
as darkness tunnels in
gripped tightly, spasms and jerking,
biting gently on a bottom lip
with pretty brown eyes
rolled back in rapture.

spur of the moment
chance encounters

snatched pleasures by moonlight,
clothes pulled to the side in haste and lust,
to fall in a heap by a barmkin,
roll off spent into sweet smelling straw,
shake loose the gold from her hair.

*

Stiff-stepped avian clerics
Balanced on a bower
While Cheviot's dreaming
Smudged in grey cloud.
Northumberland a dry husk
Blown over barley stubble,
Invaded by land rovers and SUVs
The crowds on the streets
Outside a chippy, an invasion,
A Cornish groan under weight of numbers
Heavy as a star.
The tranquility descends
With the orange and pink of the setting sun
And the hedgerows sigh
And the gentle chatter of cuddy ducks
And the crisp ripple of barnacles
On rock.

A half moon between two stars.

A stellar shock of impermanence
And the emptiness of insignificance
Sure as the incoming tides
Yet you are always there
dangled at the end of a rope
And spinning as a fly on
A silvery length of web
Wet with morning dew.

Clan of the white stag.
Deer jumping a fence
To duck behind the dunes
Nose high and graceful trot.
We are a feeling of unease on a moor
A black shadow in the woods
That raises the hackles on a terrier's back.
These ghosts soft and worn
As old denim, comfort on a hillside
Of greens and swaying trees
Howled in hollow wind
Off the North.

The caa from high perches
Of worn timber
Mocked with a belly filled
By eyeballs and flesh and maggots.

*

Will Elliott

sunshine on a loch,
the striking blue of gaze
light as Spring skies,
the laughter and frown lines on a brow
tanned as leather by winds
on the hilltops
then darkened by the rim
of a Spanish burgonet helmet
on his raids.

To dress smart for the drop;
a brown leather jack for style
as much as protection,
lip turned up in disdain
squelching over mud outside a tower door,
churned up by sheep's dainty hooves
and blackened with muck,
trying to keep boots as clean as possible.

We might live out in the wilds of the countryside,
but there's no excuse for looking provincial;
to walk tall when frequenting
the streets of Edinburgh,

names preceding the whispered conversations,
the nervous, admiring glances,
to wear a noose on that broad neck
like a fashion statement.

*

You've a reputation to uphold
when they bandy about nicknames
like *The King of Thieves*
and *The King of the Border*
for your kinsman,
hanged and his head hacked off
in the capital
for taking black mail.

We're Tushielaw –
a long approach
up a narrow band of water
that meanders by a sparse wood
and flat valley bottom below,
shades of green in the daylight.

We're Tushielaw –
the few stones now left
vaulted in long grass,

old grooves worn in the branch
of an ash gallows tree;
a baseball bat, an axe handle,
sooty buds of velvet.

We're Tushielaw
and we will have vengeance
in this life
or the next.

*

Two hogs entwined, a hogback coffin,
and the shadow of Siward Beorn -
fairbairn of the strong arm -
cast long in spring showers,
in cattle driven from dwelling,
in a face, in a helmet with nose protector.

Norse words, Danelaw,
the dipthong and long vowels,
tight curls of fleece as Odin's beard
twisted as horn where there is no
harvest festival, no celebration
of the corn and hay.

No memory of boats
carved with dragons, carrying flame
and vengeance over seas,
but landed in hills and valleys
surrounded by woods
and wildlife
and prey.

*

At the foot of the valley, a cross,
more sword than crucifixion,
glowering grey in stone eight foot tall,
not 'Welcome to Scotland' nor 'Copshawholm'
but A.A., M.A., flexed arms in a shield,
a roadside marker, a memorial to men
presented with bull's heads at the table;
a family ridden out to raid
from sparse moors around Castleton
to the surface of the moon,
hung low and bright over fertile fields,
lined grey and pockmarked in luminosity
glinting on the helmet
of a 'man of great action and good living'
who would go on to help bust
Kinmont out of Carlisle,

those same lunar illuminations
then dazzling the black visor
on a white NASA suit
from a horse with rocket boosters,
tearing through the atmosphere
and set down to land on bare dust
and rock with a thump.

Henhead pecks and flecks blood
like a bird chucked in a cock fight,
unsheathed of hood to rake claws
in a pit of sawdust, a billow of feathers
and fibrous strands, red wattle and comb
inflated with pride and self-satisfaction
to strut through the markets and cobbles
in defiance of old Forster in Bamburgh.

A crew crowed as roosters
shouting in the sun with cracked voices
risen red in shepherd's warning;
I'll steal you the stars,
bring them home in my pocket
to shine on the table,
small silver coinage of Rome.

*

This square fortress red as rust,
stands squat and square and solid
to take a beating from hail, from rain,
from musket ball and shot,
on green farmland sweeping down
to the steam lifting off beast's backs,
lowing, packed in pasture.

The dark shapes of bats
flitting around a gin-gan at dusk,
a hedgehog on grass greyed in half light,
the spines sharp as spear points
rolled tight to avoid the Faa clay
and the hot embers of camp fires;
driven home over hills purple with heather
by fast freezing mountain streams
of huge granite boulders and scree,
past hillforts topped with tumbled stone.

*

That old familiar tingle of excitement
and Bartie saddles up to ride;
a night soft and still
with an owl hooting in trees

that rustle in gentle breeze,
a cloudless night save a few
occasionally blotting out stars
in darkness, raced over in silence;
horses trotting up a dirt track,
low whinnies and pats on their flanks
from gloved hands,
the clink of swords,
of steel helmets
being removed.

Bartie peers from small windows
to see orange flames
lighting up the darkness
somewhere in the distance,
to get out on the moors,
and hot-trod with the rest of kin,
hooves sinking in bog in the darkness,
the scent of smoke in flared nostrils,
heat on a cheekbone and
the crackle and splinter
of charred wood,
soft embers dancing in the night
and falling like snow
from a hot farm stead.

The Milburns are coming.

Find the wives and bairns,
check no-one is too badly hurt
and ask who carried out the raid.

The Elliots or the Armstrongs
riding in from over the Border.

The Halls and Potts
chancing their arm over the wilds
from the neighbouring valley in Redesdale
or the Grahams
lifting forty head of beast
and driving them back into Cumberland.
No matter.

You hit them back with interest;
burn one farm and we'll fire three.
Lift eighty cattle
and we'll take back two hundred.
Hang two and we'll butcher six in return.

And so it goes on.
And so it has always been.
Retribution.

Raid.
Counter-raid.
Blood feud.

It is all about honour and respect, you see.

The Milburns are coming.

*

Ill Drooned as I never went under,
walked away from charges dry
as the sandpaper in a birdcage,
laughing the air out of my lungs,
not gurgled in cold river water
nor the dark peaty murk of a murder hole.

No barnacles on the head,
nor whelks on the tongue or seaweed for hair,
walking straight out of nightmares
in boots that don't squelch on moss,
to pour whisky down the gullet
hot as a gutful of minnows.

Ill Drooned by the Liddle or Esk,
master of Tyne, walking on ripples,

on white rapids above runs of spawning fish,

appearing through cold morning mist

as haunting as the apparition

of a man falling underwater

in suspended grace.

*

A monument to Maponus

a gathering point for raids,

for invasion parties,

that touched and slapped

the cool smooth granite

of the Lochmaben stone;

Maponus, a severed, bearded head,

floating high above blue Solway Firth

tumbled, tipped and rolled

over fields bloodied in battle,

among clouds gray as pigeons

heavy with rain,

invoked from the underworld

by hunters with flint arrowheads

for magic, for poetry,

a shrine in stone circle

at the arse end of a country

forgotten and gone;

the springs have run dry,
the dedications overgrown in bramble thorn,
so meet at the stone and ride on,
the air over Gretna black
with the hypnotic shifting shapes
of starlings excited at roosting.
Curled like an adder basking on limestone
with black diamonds on a scaled back,
forked tongue and a venomous bite,
the summer brings sunshine and showers,
animal husbandry and crops,
to tend to the farm and fill bellies with food
before the raiding returns in earnest.

*

The snow falling in flurries over Gimmerknowe
and riders wrapped in grey blankets on horseback,
flakes clagged on wool, in beards,
two horsemen appearing in gloom over old Rothbury,
silhouettes on escarpments,
to descend gingerly down tracks between dead heather,
filled wet and muddy, brown stains on white trails.

Sky dark as rooftops in rain,
the Coquet forded below Gallowfield,
meadows of thistle and gorse,

and head up the slopes of Simonside
to thieve stock, so find dark hidden crevices,
hibernate in clefts of rock, the silent cracks
in drystone walls.

*

The names traverse the lines,
sure as blood;
the church cannot help nor hinder,
no religious icons provide petition to God,
no saints with silver halos.
Adam, Walter, John…
the white in a beard, thistle down,
downturned slope of a brow
heavy ridged and solid as basalt
under a wide hat, in worn three piece tweed,
leading a horse from water with a barrel
from gamekeeper to keeper of the castle,
home of the Hotspur and enemy in
stars spun warm on a heel;
Cam doon frae they wahls…
the worn yellow sandstone
and lion rampant high over a village,
ridden in down valleys of scree
and fast burns to hit quick and hard

where faces live long,
the names as remembered
as the pious.

*

We consider our fates in oubliettes
cold stone pits darker than a November night
in Bewcastle wastes,
this is the west of soft rains
and golden sundown in fingers
over hills flattened north of Lakeland,
to think on short bark in full blossom
to fruit ripened in crisp bite
of skin and sand as hunger
turns ribs to a whippet, lean, taunt,
at the steam from the kitchens
and footsteps crept in
by wooden trapdoors above.

Kidnap and ransom,
then run to the South
to flee justice, captured in London
and brought back to contemplate
in red sandstone a whole family marked
for removal; a surname erased
by the rope, by drowning

and across water to Ireland.

The sun rising again over Esk
pink and copper, salmon and
counterfeit coin.

*

Call bills at Truce days,
flags flapping in the wind around tents
on the barren tops at Kershope Burn
and wait years for them to be settled,
the official stuff between the Wardens.

And they're all there,
drinking and joking,
looking across at the faces
of the Scottish gangs on the other side,
all the names
– the Armstrongs, the Elliots,
the Nixons and Crosers,
the Kerrs and the Scotts,
waiting for charges to be called
and deals to be done.

Nepotism, corruption,
jobs for the boys, protection rackets,

pay the black meal
and you might not burn;
we look after our friends
on the wet West frontier,
so deal with it.

*

A Croser, a shepherd's crook
hooked on the neck of a lamb
pulled clear from bog struggle
to bleat and kick free, leap in
feral glee, run for the safety
of an agitated ewe.

A Croser, a cow's smacked arse
rumbled into field corners in
see-saw gait, placid beasts
stirred to action, the dark eyes
of a bullock rolled to whites
and snorting.

A Croser, a fox scattering chickens,
jaws snapped like a gin trap, a herd
scattered by a loose dog leaping
then turned to butt and ram, panic

in the pasture, fright on the field.

A farmhouse in flames.

*

We ride in family gangs
from poor parcels of land
overgrown with thistles,
nettles, docken,
hoof prints trailed in mud,
dried coo pats on grass,
from towers curved and solid
of pink granite in the sun
like a backside on the hill.

Swallows skimming over fields
smooth as a pebble rippling water,
then rising in delight of flight,
to be captured on a arm in blue ink,
a girl's head in a star, a clan crest;
dipped and whipped above crops
swaying like the surge of a crowd
on the banked up concrete of a terrace.

Tell jokes, take the mickey,
lighten the load to an African-bound
bird in the air.

*

The Cheviots are frontiers
of tough grass and rock,
waterfalls rushing down ravines
to bubble white in pools
and hush in the winds
and the rivers,
the hills both protection and prison,
hemmed in and looming
but home.

Cheviot solitude, morose as mascara
run down the cheeks of a girl
with heels in her fingers
in Quayside night light,
distant laughter and music dulled
in neon rain reflections on a road,
a wild goat, a solitary golden eagle
hanging up high.

Take comfort in silence;

in the calm canter of uncles and brothers,

the tight embrace of the humps,

and the crags,

the dizzying elevations.

*

Mix old remedies from plants;

tell mysteries of the brown man of the moors,

and the half-man, half-goat creatures

that run down the valley of a night

kicking pots and pans out of cupboards,

strange legends of the Northern wilderness -

a black dog, a bogle, a brown dwarf;

so place a coin in milk,

rub a spelk from a gibbet on gums to cure toothache,

walk three times around the Draag stone.

High, square grey rock on tangled hillside

by black glacial lake, dropped by melt and thaw,

dark as an image painted of Burn.

Away with the preacher

who needs a god

when you've got Robert Kerr?

All those lasses breathing heavy,
breasts rising hard in loose farm garb,
lips pressed together and kissing back deeply,
tongue wet in mouth.
Tearing at clothing, exposing skin,
hands run over thighs, the gasps and moans.
And it's fast and frantic, sunk up to the hilt,
the squelch like a blade in a body and yearning,
an aching, a build up to release,
lights flashing behind closed eyes.

And seventeen souls for the death of a brother,
seventeen Collingwoods felled by the sword.
A plague on the house of Selby,
of Armorer and Ord;
a septic scab oozing puss on Norham,
a festering stench on the water of Tweed.

Risen from slumber in a bitter stone cell
to dangle from rope in morning fog
coming in thick with North Sea fret,
to become a cold spot, a shiver,
a feeling of dread and misery;
an orb captured on camera.

*

I am the last hanged man
swinging from a gibbet
the creak of rope on oak
weighted with defeat.

*

held behind glass
yellowed as piano keys
or nicotine bar-room ceilings
Watt's twisted bull horn
etched with the initials of riders
carved with a knife
and blackened with age;
lain silenced in quiet corridors
of Japanese tourists with cameras
and kids on school trips,
awaiting the press of lips
to blow and ring out,
to stir silent spirits to rise,
rustle trees of red autumn fall
and quiver like a kestrel's wings
by the side of the A1.
one blast to wake up old Edinburgh,
one blast for the Scotts

and the Whitehaugh Armstrang
- if you had fower legs,
you'd not stand there lang.

*

Sons of the stag
a red deer snorting in rut,
antlers cracked like snapped branches
in a forest, driven by bloodlust,
by blood feud,
to uphold the honour
of the family name;
horn scars on fresh saplings
that won't be healed over
by new bark.

If you want your grandfathaa's sword back,
Buccleuch,
you'll have to come to Tynedale
and take it.

A falling dream;
being chased in dreams,
that bloody sword, nothing but bother,
hung high in on wall at Hesleyside hall.

Amo, we love.
the blade last used
to cut wedding cake.

*

Grey cloth in folds as arms at an altar,
Isabella Hoppringle, Abbess of Coldstream,
carting the clergy from a field like
meat out the back of a butcher's shop
when you heard Tam Kerr was made Abbot
at Kelsae, the only ones that would grumble
tangled up in that pile for the pit.

Watched as Walter Scott of Branxholm
wiped blood from his mail, brow smeared brown,
looked down from above as
George Hoppringle of Torwoodlee
sent his horses into Edinburgh
to get the Kerrs and Homes out after
they'd stabbed him in a darkened street.

Saw Geordie of the Tanelaw
ride away from Whittingham
up over the moors driving sheep

and untangled a cross in fidgeting fingers,
whispered benedictions.

*

Did you strip a pig's back for your face
as some macabre disguise, for a laugh,
to get a rise? eye holes cut in the fat,
stiff blonde hairs protruding like some mad moonshine
hillbilly in an American horror movie
with no chainsaw but a sword,
eerie as a baegie lantern, a hellish scarecrow
out in ploughed fields, driving sheep
through a gate,
then left up in roof rafters,
tanned and leathered as a gimp mask,
to become a strange find for a museum,
an exhibit in a seaside fairground freak show,
or did you just work the hides into jacks,
stitched and sewn in flickering light,
those dexterous hands hacky
with blood and soil and muck
and stinking of pork.

*

There is no ohm on the border,
the sound of our vibration is more *Prodigy*
than finger cymbals and sitar,
more menacing than deep bass throbs
and rave stabs pulsing in laser lit darkness;
maybe it's the fault lines
running three miles underground
rumbled and rived, seams of pink shells,
fossilised fish in tunnels
by compressed stagnant forest
cut by giant blades, once hewed by hand,
now silent, driven off the farms and underground
in black donkey jackets and pit helmets,
thrown on the belt to surface
with your heritage, strong muscles flexed
by shovel not sword
out of darkness into blue skies
coal smoke tingeing the air at tea time,
a grandma fobbing off rabbit as chicken,
pulling rhubarb from garden ash.

The dust gets ingrained in your skin
and each scar becomes a tattoo
that your back marra can't scrub out.

The grime running down your eyes
like mascara at the end of a drunken hen-night,
the blackness washed around feet
and swirling down the drain hole
as one of the lads strikes up a chorus
of 'Blue Suede Shoes'
that echoes around the showers
to laughter.
Not swallows, nor pin-ups,
but lines from the belt and graft
indelibly marked forever.

*

Stowlugs is an old tupp with a gammy leg
following sheep tracks worn over years
up the steep side of hills
to summit on igneous outcrop
and purvey all in winds; red bracken,
purple heather and thistle,
ice age deposits of grey rock.

Stowlugs is slippery
as a slow worm's smooth scales,
or a glass eye, or the ice on a murder pool.
Stowlugs is hard as a horseshoe

with a nip like a horsefly,

and gans to sleep counting sheep

in hill tongues - yan, tan, tethra.

Stowlugs is a hot poker

branding an arse cheek,

an apparition, a magpie hopping on thatch,

the electric static afore thunder,

a bearskin pelt, mushrooms and mould

on Gilsland, on a crop stalk,

a drink warm with vomit and bile,

poppies and psilocybin.

Stowlugs is the laugh of a madman rocking,

sea washing up and pebbles

and rushing back, lunar pull,

the hoot of a hoolit, a clump

off a donkey, a headbutt,

a bitten ear, a wild goat by a cairn,

a fish leaping rapids, a tick

on the black nose of a ewe,

a gaggle of seagulls at dawn.

Stowlugs is at the door.

*

Hexham is a dangerous place for a mosstrooper;
the biscuit sandstone of the jail
standing squat and square
with mean slits of windows
where no light can penetrate the gloom
contained within dungeons.

The gateway and the Moothall
where the bailiff resides,
the impressive Abbey once smashed
and pillaged by distant ancestors
of the Norse Great Heathen Army;
Halfdan Ragnarsson, Björn Ironside,
Ivar the Boneless and Sigurd Snake-in-the-Eye,
who wreaked the countryside
with sword and terrible vengeance
in the thick grey fog of history
long before the riders.

The seats of authority,
the town full of sworn men,
prickers for the Commission
with their bloodhounds
to scour the surrounding hills and dales

for fugitives and broken clansmen.

Hexham never forgets.
Stone blackened by Scottish fire
and sword wounds cut deep
into lineage of fathers and sons
who aren't quick to forgive
and forget past wrongs.

Tynedale carries the scars
like an old fighting dog,
whitened and hardened over,
bow-legged, tough and resilient
with a purposeful snarl.

Hexham is where the North Tyne
meets the South Tyne,
a melting pot for the families
from all around.

The Ridleys riding in from Haltwhistle,
the Carnabys and Fenwickes,
all arriving in small groups,
adding to an ever-growing
boisterous atmosphere
on the cobbles outside an ale house.

*

The plague's in at Newcastle,
at Hexham and Berwick,
they're dropping in Carlisle,
on Teviot and Merse,
each cough a suspicion,
fingers pressed under armpits
to seek out lumps, feel the cold
sweats, the fevers, a trickle of blood
from a nose, the sickness, wet diarrhoea,
weak aching bones and black toes.

Sickness knows no border,
gold is no good if you've dropped your guts
and spewed up your lungs in pink panic,
so head back to the bastles on Esk,
stay shut behind oak doors 'til it passes,
pile bodies in plague holes and pray;
your name is no use to you now.

*

On nights when lightning flashes
over the looming presence of dark hills
and thunder rumbles around the valley

so low that you feel it in your chest,

your very being,

you go up to a child's room,

ruffle his stuck-up blonde hair and tell him:

remember you're a Charleton, son.

Fear nothing;

you've the blood of legends

running in your veins.

Jerry 'Topping' Charleton.

Cokes Charleton.

Lionel Charleton of Thornburgh.

Thomas Charleton, the laird of Howkupp.

Kin and clan.

The great thieves of Tynedale, tamed.

*

March Law, the only Law on the Border.

The sheer will and determination

of battle-hardened, violent men

to protect what they have

and take what they can.

A silver spur served for dinner.

*

Jock Pott the bastard

blacker than a shag with wings outstretched

like crucifixion on white pillars of Farne;

body bloated, an Atlantic seal

basked on a bed as the fizzing North Sea

running off sands and igneous outcrops,

in bladderwort and seaweed,

underwater echo and swell,

the hills like new denim in distance;

Northumberland, a bottle

over the back of the head,

a St. George tabard inside out to turncoat.

There's no dragon in these hills but a Pott,

bent and salted beach wood

piled and pyred as broken skeletons

in a kist, a cairn atop slopes

laden with bilberries,

purple stains of bird droppings,

cuckoo spit on a blade of grass,

Jock Pott cocooned in white bubbles,

in the small pebbles on mayfly nymphs

dragged over orange river bottoms

of silt, and at Yardhope, a shepherd in plaid,

stolen sheep in a pen on nights
where someone smashed a circuit board
and slotted it in sky.

*

Stand tall with a snarling black dog
stood out alone from battle lines
to single combat at Halidon hill;
a kinsman, the same blood and bone
as broken by an English axe,
both dog and master split in two
like dry kindling,
old champions of the Scottish nation
still riding in high pastures
to descend on Alwinton in a pack
breaking soft birdsong in hedgerows
with screams, the terror rising in
animals scattered to run widly,
spuggies scattered in a mass
of applause, the smoke rising up
in a valley.

*

a creosote gate, moon on pale grass
gallowfield, gallowbrae,
an iron yett hammered into a plough
that cuts a way through stars and galaxies
viewed from an observatory,
blacker than coal or a hole
so you don't see the hills
but sense them
looming and brooding.

the gurgle of a burn, silvered stream,
baa at a dyke edge,
winter air tingled skin and frozen breath
high lunar illuminated shapes of sheep huddled
by hedgerows, hard molehills on grey.
frost crystallising on dry stone,
on barren branches, the crunch underfoot.

every astral movement
recorded in rings and cups on rock.

*

Romans built the Wall
hundreds of years ago,
from square stone blocks
cut straight through Charleton land
to follow the line of Whin Sill;
huge pillars of volcanic rock
jutting out of the earth
and tilted by time.

There's not a farm in the dale
that hasn't got at least part of its buildings
constructed by stone lifted from the wall.
Whey, you'd be stupid not to.

Secret shrines in the countryside,
hidden in among the snarling brambles
and green shade of trees,
marked with Latin letters.
To play there as children,
follow gurgling burns
into the undergrowth.

Never put stock in religion.
Topping wrecked ten churches,

or so it's been told,
just for the devilment;
because he could.

Nothing to do with God,
just to winde up Archbishops.
It's all about power
and the rich pickings
in silver goblets and plates.

Do not fear God;
what's his surname anyway?
that's all that matters around here.
If he's not a Robson, a Milburn,
a Dodd or a Charleton,
then he is nothing, simple as that.

No supreme being sits in judgement.
It is Kings and Queens
that decide fate for good or ill;
Royalty
or Northumberland
or one of the Fenwickes.

We hold our own services,
serve our own stolen wine.

*

The name that once afforded me protection
is now a noose around my neck.
I cannot go and serve some powerful landowner,
take orders from a man not of a surname.
I'd rather die in my boots
than cower on my knees.
Do you know nothing of respect?

Stick your Scotland up your arse,
your tartan highlanders,
misty lochs and glens and Saint Andrew.
Stick England up there too;
the ruffled neckpieces,
the Yorkshire dales,
the Minster and Saint George.
I'm Northumberland and will always be.

I cannot flee and become anonymous
in some southern English town
or across in Ireland,
changing my name and not reacting
when they hear my odd tongue
and accuse me of being a Scot.
The suspicion of strangers,

the stories of lawless wild men and women.

I'm Northumberland, you ignorant get,
listen to the cadences in my voice.
If it wasn't for the Dodds,
the Scots would have over-run
England centuries ago.

Men forged by Kings
and their lust for command,
the unquenchable thirst for more coin,
yet looked down on in disgust,
the rabble with barbaric customs.

Tarset and Tarret Burn,
hard and heather bred, yet, yet, yet.
To it, Tynedale!

*

Bust out of Swinburne Castle
then locked up at York, in chains,
after another attempted jailbreak;
smashing the bars and leaping the walls
for a boat on the Ouse,
where Sim Armstrong cowped an ankle

fresh air blowing hair
exuberant as a horse in full gallop,
Cessford's henchmen – Ralph Burn,
Will Tait, Dandy Pringle,
Robert Frissell, Richard Rutherford,
legs pumping furiously in atmosphere
to land with a thud and roll
on dewed slopes, to tumble
with Buccleuch's pledges in a heap,
the wind knocked from Will Elliott
like a knife piercing haggis;
back out and saddled up again
to cross the Cheviots for Glendale,
to put the crowned head of King James
on the table with a thud,
a crested shield on the reverse,
an Irish harp, the Scottish lion,
to lift a sheep
and sod the law.

*

Where Kings failed to shift us, cash will out;
a farm labourer can't buy his house
for quarter of a million, so we'll haunt
barn conversions, turn land once grazed

now golf course to dust, crack brick
and rot the rafters of the roofs.
Harry Hotspur the hero, the protector,
his armour rusted and spurs blunted
to a property developer in a sharp suit,
the hooves to rumble around hills
in thunder, faces lit by lightening,
names still whispered by wheatfields.

Mick Pott dispossessed,
the overnight cells empty and echo,
weight lifted from villages
twinkling with orange streetlights
in the black cleft of valleys;
whole crews dispersed
like dandelion seeds in the wind
to Yorkshire, to Surrey,
to Lanzarote.

*

Plaster damp on red block by a stairwell
hacked off with a nicker
to reveal your name, long forgotten and hidden,
lightly covered by key marks,
yet defiant and bold;

ARTHVR
GRAME
MOT
cut in with a chisel head high
chipped and chinked into stone,
into history, with the skill
of a craftsman.

Carlisle castle, clammy, dank,
attacked by the rain, by the Scots,
soft drizzle on a window
by the jambs where you leaned
and looked out over the city.

No Perspex to keep fingers off
the cold touch of stone worn smooth,
no celebration, no boards,
neglected as graffiti
by a crest of John Comyn,
three sheaves of corn,
two helmeted heads,
a spun wheel.

Dragged off to boats at Workington
with three quid in your pocket,
drab beaches of mud and pebble

to look back at the Solway,
the mountains rising,
and on out to sea and the rain.

To hell with Roscommon,
you never left home.

*

Saddle up and meet again
at some quiet spot near the Border
under darkness,
silent save the horses' heavy breathing,
and set out to drive home beast
over the moors from an English farm
not knowing if you'll meet resistance
or bump into a raid
heading in the other direction.
The thrill of the black;
nocturnal skies lit only
by strange galaxies and stars,
the moon looming large and luminous
pitted by craters.

The talk is of survival now.
Of who has gone to the gallows

and who could be next.
Of conscription to Ireland
and land being seized by the Crown,
the bastards on the Commission
and tough justice.

Davie Irving, tortured at the races
by men not of a riding surname
holding the leather halters
of fine animals, all kicking,
snorting and straining at the bit,
sinewy and shiny in the sunshine;
a horse to get you over the hills and home
for if you can't ride, you can't raid.

*

Arrived in invasion and fighting
Harle of Normandy, this Union of Crowns
brings winners and losers on flat fields
around Redesdale, risen to rough moors,
a reputation as bad as the Grahams
yet unlevied, stealing beast and sheep
with fleece white as Mad Jack's wig
left at Alnwick court in haste
to join the Jacobite uprising.

A magistrate with temper
hotter than camp fire coals, flashed
like blowback then dispersed,
who would reckon on talking his way home;
the dulcet Northumbrian tones
uneasy in a London ear, sped in frustration,
his dubious honour
last to be hung, drawn and quartered
at Tyburn for high treason in 1716,
grey spirit still stalking the corridors
of Otterburn Hall, the initials carved
over an entrance.

Or battled at a Flotterton BBQ,
knocked over tables and marquee shook
as Party Marty and his brothers
let loose with stone quarryman's fists,
old animosity honoured,
the Coquet and Rede bloodied
to a Heavy Metal soundtrack.

*

Head to higher sheilings to weather this now,
dark clouds suddenly appearing
on a warm day in the Cheviots,

to be hammered by hailstones
big as pebbles.

Then calm as the black skies break
and sunrays bathe the hills golden,
shafts from the heavens lighting up green.

Livestock gathered in the corner of a field
with heads hung low dripping water,
frozen balls caught in wool,
grouped up against stonework
with backs to the wind.

Sheltered by limestone walls
curved into circles, protected by Redesdale,
the sanctuary of wide empty moors,
the woods, the waters,
the dank refuge of an abandoned bastle,
a breeze whistled through windows
and the flicker of small flame.

*

Stones blackened by water
piled haphazard on bog and marsh,
the red tails of squirrels in conifers
by forestry tracks battered by wind,

curlew cries on desolate moorland
near grassy humps of old founds,
clumps of rock and lime mortar,
the mosses and lichen reclaiming
walls once warmed now greened over,
and the roofs are long gone,
cowped in and exposed to the elements,
bracken, and branches, and frogspawn,
rotting vegetation and the gurgle of burns;
leave a coin on the lintel
as tribute.

*

Northumberland is over-run with tourists,
narrow pavements as infuriating
as the aisles of a Sainsburys,
backed up and stopped
and stepped around and forced onto roads
by aged incomers with holiday homes.
Blame Robson Green.
Blame Harry Potter.
Driving 30 miles an hour up the A1
in a tailback behind three campervans,
two caravans and a sconehunter
in an immaculate Volvo, to beaches now filled

with kites and bodyboards and the high
stench of dog shite; old weather-beaten
castles invaded by members of
English Heritage in Bear Grylls' gear,
get your pants taken down for a can of pop,
bent over for a stottie, house prices
driving people off the land quicker
than a Scottish invasion force or the plague;
the kicking now weaker than the last
shadows on the gallows, in resignation, defeat,
there is no fight left, no riot, no raising
the names, drained to the cities
nigh gone.

*

To be a mosstrooper off a riding surname
makes you a law unto yourself.
You can forget England and Scotland.
forget the Wardens, the March Laws,
the only loyalty is to the heidsman,
the family name.
To be part of a crew.
A notorious rider.
Respected.

That's what they could never quite grasp

in Edinburgh or London.
Will Elliot follows no flag but his own.
There are no three lions of England
or lion rampant of Scotland,
just the crests of Kings
that mean nothing to a yeoman farmer
in the border wilderness
of tangled heather,
where we've stolen beast for beef,
sheep for mutton and profit,
raided houses,
wreaked havoc on towns
in the *name* of the crowns only.

But we did it for ourselves.
Purely for ourselves;
a powerful man gets rich,
a poor man watches his crops burn.
It's the natural order of things.

Who needs a King when you're an Elliot?
You can wipe your arse
on the flags of St. George and St. Andrew
for all Will Elliot cares.

That's why Buccluech and Hume
turned their backs on their followers
and threw in their lot with the King.
Will didn't condone it,
but he understood it.
It was all about self-preservation.
Especially now.

The banished back from Ireland in droves,
the rabble returned,
right hands unblessed by a christening,
no fear of holy retribution.

*

Late August and the shadows start to lengthen,
and the nights are cutting in,
sun feeble above the curve of hills;
sheep down off high pasture
to graze on wide haughs sharp with gorse,
by shingles on shallow water thirsty
for fresh flow from the mountains
to lead a flash of silver
home to spawn and rot.

The towers and crow steps of red Jeddart,
Royal Burgh and the Abbey,
step off trails of grass and dust to cobble,
off river valleys cut through sandstone
by trees and escarpments and peles
to hold your head high in steel helmet,
to walk through streets brazen
in both name and reputation.

Take a knife to dice mutton and trim fat,
blade edge sliced through sinew to peel away bone
white as the heads of a sitting of old gentlemen
that hear tales of misdeeds in oak chambers.
Drop a cleaver on wood,
the meat is most sweet when it's stolen.

Break out of fox cover to run, to put your nose
in air sweet with meadow dew, to snap cobwebs
glinting with moisture in morning mist
before burn off.
The hounds are sniffing around the fields,
in a howling pack, John Tait, and small birds flit
from hedgerow to hedgerow in chattering flocks.
A herd of fat wedders tearing at grass,
rabbit bounding away with the flick of white tail,
grey smudge of hills in the distance;

whether the red of a todd or hair of a reiver
in bracken and heather,
the sheep are up-kittled to fitful bleat.

We are the undead, the unhanged or drowned,
the unfled to the West, to gather in harvest,
reap golden crops not trampled by armies
nor fired and black as sheep droppings
in long swishing grass. We're off Scott-free.
We're geese with leaden feet.

*

An underwater echo of voices,
the sight of legs as if through a fish eye
and the bubbles of breath escaping
garbled in panicked head and burning lungs.

To be held under a pool
dark with peat and mountain run-off
rotting leaves and mulch;
water is cheaper than rope.

Flapping like a salmon on muddy banks,
Bold Jock's a strange fish
to be hauled up dripping from Nith,

no need for a priest to bash brains in.

Hair plastered wet to his heid,
eyes cold as a haddock on ice,
not gutted nor picking small bones
but bloated by river, and blue.

*

A phantom on a dark horse
forewarning danger.

A spectral vision thin as mist
appearing to passing cars, a post bus,
one hand holding his side.

Robert Snowdon was just 16
when he killed the Scottish champion John Grieve
in single combat at Gammelpath.

Twice returned as the Coquet burst its banks
and threatened to flood Hepple
like a long forgotten memory recalled in a dream
and you're unsure whether it really happened
or you made it up, or déjà vu,
or just some weird phenomenon
of electric static and water,

some strange paranormal event that you want to believe;
the rider still protecting his village.

The black horse recovered in cold trod
and knifed in the ribs for his trouble,
now whinnied and reared up by brown and red hills,
his ancestors still brandishing the sword,
still watched over and waiting.

*

The nights are dark and still
as a town smothered in snow
in Northumberland,
save when the wind howls in
off the wild North Sea.

So you didn't make too much noise;
the crack of twigs pricking the ears
of nocturnal meandering
badgers and foxes,
alerting distant dogs to bark an alarm.

Out in the blackness of the tight trees,
moonlight glimmering
between breaks in the canopy,

a church appearing at the edge of the cover,
spectral and silent in the gloom,
peering out from gnarled trunks
like pine martens,
cursing in whispers,
and holding back sniggers.

The thrill of the night,
wearing planets and constellations
as a cloak, as the feathers of starlings.

*

William Cockburn of Henderland,
near neighbour of the King of Thieves,
fellow Ettrick rider who embarked
on many raids with Adam Scott,
his face scarred by battle
that only a mother could love
with a milky eye,
jagged white scarring,
bad teeth and rough stubble;
beheaded by the King at Edinburgh
in 1529.

And you, his namesake, his distant kinsman,
now led to the gallows with a Graham
for lifting a horse in family tradition,
feeling the choke and the burn
as you kick like a fresh foal,
then dangle and swing
limp as a weak man's handshake
on a boring Tuesday in summer.

Look back one last time
at the Coquetdale hills in the distance,
the curves of the ridges beyond,
the Border, on into Scotland, and wonder,
did he collect you as a wraith,
did he forewarn you of the end?

A wraith gathers a decedent
whatever the distant connections,
paternal blood pumped into limbs
or splattered on the brown furrows
of ploughed ground
whether in the green valleys
of Teviot or Tyne.

It's time to go;
onwards, into the unknown.

*

His father took him poaching for fish
when he was younger;
there wasn't a Young around
that couldn't tickle a trout out of a burn.

To head down to the river
to old spots where they'd lain
on the bank and slipped arms
into icy cold water,
hands softly stroking
the weight of a fish's belly,
tender as caressing a woman.

The South Tyne lapping up
gently against the sides,
swirling in dark brown pools
and picking up momentum
as it became a torrent
down into a slow moving
but powerful pull
at Hexham, where the waters met.

The rush of the river
and the chirping of birdsong
providing some comfort.
Taking a fish from the water
never felt like stealing to Thomas.
Mind, lifting cattle and sheep
never felt like theft either;
nor riding up to produce a flintlock
and stick it in the face of a carriage man.

So as you await them tying that rope
around your neck, Tom Young,
think on the stillness, the birdsong,
think on the calmness of waters,
think on of hyem.

*

It's always a thin, raw wind
when the Cheviot tops are white as a gimmer's back
and the clouds come in down river valleys
tumbled with gliders of smooth stone,
topped by tangles of bramble and bracken.

A bleak Thursday in November,

Thorsday, and the hammer's falling down,
grey and washed out as the swirl
of turps in a paint pot,
with frost on the grass, frozen soil
cold as steel gate posts
or the plough
behind a cow byre.

Breath rising like the bleat of stolen sheep
or the fog over deep salmon pools
black with peat,
icicles and wiry wool on a barb;
skeletons of dark dead trees
stark as a gibbet.

John Scott, chilled to chattering teeth,
to grimace at the noose
for forty-eight rams and a ewe lifted
from Sim Dodd at Elsdon;
sword marks still etched
in the stone pillars of the church,
those same bloody cuts
of Dodd the elder's ancestors,
saddled up for a raid and red hand,
a hot trod from Redesdale,
and they're risen.

Bonny Lizzy Charleton found it a thrill
to get strangled during sex,
dark hair stroked back behind her ears
as she gave little gasps of pleasure,
nipples hardening,
slippery as eels between her thighs.
Begging for rough hands
on her smooth skin,
squeezing until she'd almost passed out.

On Fairmoor, a bus stop now,
in a copse of trees,
by the road
near a mental hospital.
The green of wide fields,
Simonside and the Cheviot tops
dusted with soft fall and hail,
the North Sea grey as coping stones
with chop.
No birdsong, no curlew cry,
just the bleak whistle of the winds
and the mumble of a minister.

Bonny Lizzy's lover
was a sadistic torturer named

John Sage of Chillingham Castle.
A moonlit masochistic session
on the wrack went badly wrong
and Sage killed her by mistake.
The heidsmen sent word to the King
that if Sage wasn't executed himself
they'd join forces with the Teviotdale riders
to burn Chillingham
and decimate the countryside around.
The threat was enough.

Coarse hemp itchy against stubble,
gulping as the adam's apple chokes up
to obstruction, to feel the apprehension
stirring deep in the guts.
A Bellendaine! and fire the Rede,
the histories entwined like two adders
basking on a rock,
an infinity snake, a blue tattoo,
a grandfather's stolen sword.

Sage, his face dark
with indignant rage,
was strung up
and the crowd
cut off pieces of flesh

for strange souvenirs
as he was still kicking.
Pulling out knives to hack
at a finger, or an ear,
and laughing at the spinning body
of the once feared executioner
who had rolled Scots' prisoners around
in barrels of spikes for fun.

There's nae shame in stealing sheep,
John Scott,
last of the clan
to hang for the crime,
the last to go now
and join the ranks of proud thieves
that dangled before you.

The rope drops and tightens;
You're in Bonny Lizzy ecstasy.

*

This is the land of no sun;
of skies dark as puddle water,
weird electric storms and Northern lights,
where the bleating of animals means trouble.

This is our land, our home.
Nights haunted by the chill of riders
emerging from fog and sea fret,
from the clefts of hills and cover of trees.

A green man of mosses, of shore sand
and mud churned up by a cattle trough,
in silence by drystone dykes, down valleys
wet with dew and hidden in hillforts,
jackets whipped by wind, the pressure in ears
strained for sound.

Where you stand above the clouds
and they close in thick as plaid, the moisture
akin to a boat on the North Sea, tasted,
rocked and rolling down hobbled tracks
worn by fell runners, sheep, hikers.

On grey lintels of lichen the
strange cannibal spiders in dark moleskin
feast on arachnids, adders lay curled on stone,
a family of wild goats wander moors, the horns
an old Billy worn as bark carved in the top
of a gatepost.

A rumble of horses untamed, to whinny
with eyes rolled to whites, spooked out
from bracken and birch. We build walls thick
and keep the doorway up a ladder
so you can't scumfish us out. The thump
of a bolt pulled shut, my home
is my castle, my pele, my bastle.

Get oot and keep oot.

*

Hand me St. John's head on a plate.
These healing plants on the green slopes of the side of the river;
picked and tugged from the earth and ground in a pestle
smooth as a Tari coin, worn by many hands, John's long curls
and a platter.
Jerusalem in Coquetdale, our sacred order,
No dusty streets, yellowed in sand and dirt, no shaking palms
or calls to prayer;
just the wind rustling in trees and a fox,
nose tilted to the air for the scent of danger.
Our green church, white cross on a red flag,
flapping on a hillside by the gallows.

Shadows of the Knights Hospitaller,
an ancient tradition

grey as the morning mists
that snake down the valley;
old stones tipped and cowped over,
then hidden in long grass
at Physic Lonnen.

*

Close down the wards, shut the doors.
Lock out that cold Coquet wind bringing snow
in white flurries over Simonside,
bolted and silent.

Stalk stark corridors like the creeping frost
crystallising long grasses by the river edge
and pools that flash silver with a trout's steady side,
turned and then settled on gravel.

The touch of a caring hand to memory
as a hand that has stroked a fish flank
at times tender yet firm
then dissipated and gone, fast as rain.

Sky fat with foreboding,
once blue as a nurses' tunic now grey as concrete,
the cows huddled steaming in a muddy field corner
heads hanging low, awaiting the storm.

*

Born with backs to the wall, the stone,
the fear of Rome; Oswald, descended from Angles
and brought up on Iona,
swore vengeance for his uncle King Edwin
slaughtered by the Celtic Welsh,
marched an army
from Bamburgh to Tynedale.

The visions of Columba foretelling victory
the wall again at our backs and a wooden
crucifix to lead us; this is for Eanfrid
the brother, slain by the sword,
this is for Northumberland,
Bernicia, and a Christian God.

Faceplates and spears, the Welsh routed,
Cadwallon carved up,
hacked splashing in the Rowley Burn
the water running red
for our sacrament; the body, the blood
on Heavenfield where we go
to die.

*

Cunedda, Votadini King,
the fort of the spear shafts
and decapitation,
heads rotted as old baegies
to the white of bone, of clouds
and surf;
you will not trample us
in celebration tablets of stone.

*

Northumberland; the silver flash of a lizard
in purple heather and grey sand,
the storm clouds racing across
big skies; a tree trunk blackened by
lightening strike. Northumberland
the blood of the invader.
The Norseman, the Dane,
the Norman, a sword beating a shield.
Northumberland the glint of an Anglian hoard
in soil dark as peat.

*

Northumberland; fifty head of stolen sheep
inside the barmkin wall,
bleating and honking to high heaven,

the white moisture from wet black nostrils
rising in the air like fog.
Northumberland, warm mutton in the belly,
braxy lamb, we are a kail
of oatmeal and salted meat,
blood and pus, the flag of
St. Oswald.

*

Northumberland
you've let us down;
reform family crews in familiar hills –
the Stankford, Dow Know, Cherrytrees,
and head back over the line.
Turn around tabards, turned again,
a flimsy cross of St. George
trampled in mud, fluttered off
in high winds over Staerough
by a white trig point.

I belong to this land and a name.

When Hogg ploughed our soil,
we left him for dead;
when Priest's Will read from the pulpit
we brought down high vengeance.

No Christ but kin, no divine retribution
but Sir Robert Kerr.

*

We crossed the Border to flee Jeddart justice,
hidden in Northumberland's hills
to follow deer down the steep side of burns
in the golden glow of morning, to take fish
like an otter, gouged by the gaff,
to avoid hanging from a gibbet
or the nearest tree.

And the dawn is now purple and yellow
as eyes blackened in fist fights,
and the rain falls soft on grey slate
with hypnotic patter, the same water,
the same stars that shone over those nicknames
then driven to legend and folk law –
the Bailie, the Burgess,
the Sheriff, Spider.

We are the Anglo-Scots,
the people of mountains and dales,
harbingers of the hangman's noose
forged from frontiers and blood feud
and flame, cast down to impotent rage.

*

Hands not those of a farmer
but a thief, no calloused grip,
no honest graft nor honour in crops
trampled and burned, or stock
driven off. Who needs a plough
when you have a sword?

*

Teviotdale, home of forefathers
in dour towers of stone, laid out in lines
of grey headstones and reel off the names
like a Highlander before battle:
Jon, son of John, son of Wilfred, son of Henry,
son of Thomas, son of Robert, son of William,
son of John, son of William…to go back hyem,
back to the paintbrushes, the stone quarries,
the butcher's shop; to trade in whippets,
appear on the drunk list fighting,
the faces craggy and tilted in flat cap shadow,
fingers iced in pools to tickle a trout.

*

Ancestors waiting on sparse moorland
to heed the call and saddle up once again,
to ride slowly into high cornfields

with those that have gone before,
no fear of the mason's marks, hoisted up
onto horseback by a recognisable hand
and given a helmet; to mutter in old Dane
on the mudflats of Jutland, to watch over the bairns,
the *barns*, from the piles of cairns,
the summits over Yetholm loch.

To become a star in Orion's belt.

*

Henning of the Pirn
cast off in the longships of Jarl Birger,
hugged dragon heads of wood in waves,
salted and wet in white water.

A stag's head and stars,
Red saltire shield, to beat an axe on boards
in a terrible tattoo, seaweed tangled as the knots
in blonde Ingeborg's hair; to blood a blade
for Swedish Kings in Finland.

*

Fjords cold with mountain snow
run off in waterfalls down steep ravines.
Teitr the oarsman, the joker,

sons in Iceland, Shetland, borne from the
black North Sea and chilled by flurries of flakes.

Bubbles in grey mud pools, black volcanic sands
and the wind driving over sparse hilltops.
Sanctuary in solitude,
in the tangled branches of rookeries,
to sail into waves rising like misery
hard as an iron icon of Thor's mighty hammer.

*

A ring of Danish heads on spikes
around Durham's walls
and blood feud is nothing new;
Uhtred of Bamburgh's killer hunted down
then avenged by his sons,
and so it goes on…

Then we are the departed,
long removed from the red candy-striped strips,
the mazy runs of Michael Laudrup,
the goals of Preben Elkjaer.
The faces in a Panini sticker book,
the games on TV -
Jesper Olsen, Johnny Sivebaek,

Soren Lerby, Allan Simonsen,
Frank Arneson, Brian Laudrup,
flickering in blue on a woodchip wall,
no meadow but a trimmed field.
Bernicia, the blood of Allfather
running in veins.

*

Barearse, a granite tower on a hillside
overlooking a loch, the sheep on the
slopes where fallen stones lie, trees
bent by wind and it's gone, energy
in an empty space, a few lines
in the records, a farmer's fence, gorse and
beagie fields clagged in mud.

*

Other bastles and peles long abandoned
or incorporated in the walls of farmhouses,
vibrations recorded in rock where
the burns keep on gurgling like a drunk;
here, a sword was sharpened, here, an axe.
Some now country houses, heritage sites,
hotels; the hollow barrel of Tushielaw, the
pile of blackened stones at Mangerton, the

wind whistling over bleak moors at Kielder.
Norwegian spruce and pine, the churned up
tracks of forestry wheels, frost and ice.

*

They come riding in under night,
the men of the Commission,
led by old Selby himself.

Attempting to smash doors into splinters
with axes, purposeful shouting,
torch flames lighting up faces orange in the dark.

But the door holds;
sharp metal sunk deep into wood,
so they scumfish you out,
setting fresh hay at the door
to smoulder smoke up a staircase,
thick and choking;
a penance for those fired
on raids into Scotland.

The thumping and whacking from clubs
knocking the fight out, blood choking thick
in the throat from a blow to the nose
that flashes a blinding white light between eyes.

Taken to Westgate,
risen early and led up a narrow cobbled nick,
out of a gate up to the green rise at Gallowgate,
just outside of the City walls,
with coarse ropes dangled in preparation
that itch and scratch at necks.

No trial, no deportations.
They're going to make us all swing.

Mosstroopers from the wild hills,
that steal horses, disobey the authorities
and live and die by their own rules and codes of honour;
men that have killed Scots and done battle
in fearsome dales where none may tread
if they don't carry the right surname.

Clump up those wooden steps onto the platform
one at a time as the ropes are thrown
over a beam
and tied.

*

The faces are tinged blue.
Life choked out of them,
kicking and struggling at the end of a noose
or squeezed in the surge on a terrace,
feet lifted and forced forward into a barrier.
The panic packed tight in decrepit grounds
with peeling paint on brick
and the stench of ammonia,
fried onions, cigarettes, stale alcohol
under the tangle of a metal stanchion roof.

They wore kilts in The Corner,
Gallowgate a moving mass of pink arms
as if an anemone rolled by waves
under a scoreboard with digital men.
Hops from Scottish & Newcastle; floodlights and
cranes on a city skyline, bridges on a river,
rivets in a steel hull.
We're pitmen on a picket line,
we're a blue neon star lit on the corner
of a boisterous bar.

We're the Gremlins,
We're the Rezerection.

Prada and Stone Island, Paul Richmond Destroy,
we're a bag of speed and a handful of E's
in a dark space lit up by strobes and throbbing
with sound.

*

We are a checked shepherd's tartan,
Lindisfarne mead, smoked kippers and stotties,
Brown ale and Export, pease pudding, bilberries,
coal dust and hen nights, United,
the Charlton brothers and Jackie Milburn,
pigeon duckets, slag heaps, colliery wheels,
we're an industrial angel, a dipthong and vowels,
a city risen from slumber.

Sunday dinner at your nana's,
dart board on the scullery door,
a motorbike in the passage,
engine oil and a lighthouse at night. The orange panel
on an NCB donkey jacket, castles and battlefields.

We're this and so much more.

We are the last sons and the daughters

of the King of Thieves.

Jon Tait is a sportswriter and poet who lives on the Anglo-Scottish border. His first full collection Barearse Boy was published by Smokestack in 2017.

Printed in Great Britain
by Amazon